S0-EFM-673

WILD! Exploring Animal Habitats

CREATURES OF A
COLORFUL
CORAL REEF

Francine Topacio

PowerKiDS
press

New York

Published in 2020 by The Rosen Publishing Group, Inc.
29 East 21st Street, New York, NY 10010

Copyright 2011; revised edition 2020

Editor: Elizabeth Krajnik
Book Design: Reann Nye

Photo Credits: Cover martin_hristov/Shutterstock.com; Series Art Nechayka/Shutterstock.com; p. 5 optionm/Shutterstock.com; p. 6 Chris Holman/Shutterstock.com; p. 7 Pawe? Borówka/Shutterstock.com; p. 9 Tom Goaz/Shutterstock.com; p. 10 Damsea/Shutterstock.com; p. 11 _548901005677/Moment/Getty Images; p. 12 JonMilnes/Shutterstock.com; p. 13 Divelvanov/Shutterstock.com; p. 14 Georgette Douwma/DigitalVision/Getty Images; p. 15 Kristina Vackova/Shutterstock.com; p. 16 Kerstin Meyer/Moment/Getty Images; p. 17 Andrea Izzotti/Shuttertock.com; p. 19 Rich Carey/Shutterstock.com; p. 20 Stephen Frink/Image Source/Getty Images; p. 21 Chris Holman/Shutterstock.com; p. 22 divedog/Shutterstock.com.

Cataloging-in-Publication Data

Names: Topacio, Francine.
Title: Creatures of a colorful coral reef / Francine Topacio.
Description: New York : PowerKids Press, 2020. | Series: Wild! exploring animal habitats | Includes glossary and index.
Identifiers: ISBN 9781725304444 (pbk.) | ISBN 9781725304468 (library bound) | ISBN 9781725304451 (6 pack)
Subjects: LCSH: Coral reef ecology-Juvenile literature. | Coral reef animals-Juvenile literature.
Classification: LCC QH541.5.C7 T67 2020 | DDC 577.789-dc23

Manufactured in the United States of America

CPSIA Compliance Information: Batch #CSPK19. For Further Information contact Rosen Publishing, New York, New York at 1-800-237-9932.

CONTENTS

CORAL BASICS

What is coral? Is it a plant? An animal? A rock? Coral is an animal that sticks to the ocean floor. Even though corals may look like rocks or plants, they're animals and can't make their own food. They have **tentacles** that catch their food and put it into their mouth.

A single coral animal is called a polyp. Polyps have soft bodies and make a hard outer **skeleton** that holds them to rocks or the skeletons of other dead polyps. Some species, or kinds, of corals grow and die on top of other dead coral polyps. All these corals build the base of coral reefs.

Corals come in all shapes, sizes, and colors and grow in warm and cool waters. Hard corals build reefs. Soft corals, such as sea fans, don't build reefs.

5

BUILDING REEFS

Coral polyps that grow close together form a colony. As they live and die, their skeletons build up. Over time, large, rocky places called coral reefs form. Some of the biggest coral reefs are thousands of years old.

Coral polyps have a tiny **alga** living inside them. The alga has **shelter** and feeds on the coral's waste. The coral, in turn, feeds on the alga.

More animals live on or near coral reefs than in any other part of the ocean.

Coral reefs are often called the rain forests of the sea. Plants and animals live on reefs, visit reefs to find food, and use reefs to hide from predators. Some animals even eat coral polyps.

AT HOME ON THE REEF

Coral reefs are most often found in clear **tropical** oceans. Some animals make their homes on a reef and never leave it. Live polyps, sea anemones, and sponges live on coral reefs around the world. Sea anemones are large polyps and are closely related to coral. They are often brightly colored. However, they have poisonous stinging tentacles.

Sea sponges have lived on Earth for millions of years. They keep ocean habitats working well. Even though sponges are very simple animals, they have an important job. They take in and clean ocean water—almost 400 gallons (1,500 L) a day!

Creature Corner

Sea sponges are home to other **organisms**. Fish, sea stars, and other animals need sponges to find food, rest, lay eggs, and may even eat the sponge.

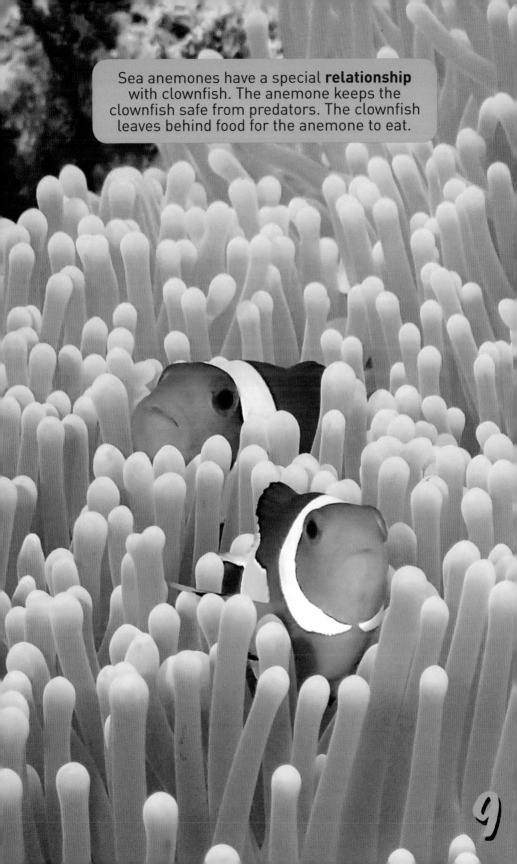

Sea anemones have a special **relationship** with clownfish. The anemone keeps the clownfish safe from predators. The clownfish leaves behind food for the anemone to eat.

9

SEA STARS

Echinoderms are invertebrates, or animals that don't have backbones, that live in the ocean. They get their name from their hard, spiny skin. Most echinoderms are round with five **symmetrical** parts. They have many tiny feet with suckers on them to help the animals move. Sea stars are echinoderms.

Creature Corner

Sea stars belong to the class Asteroidea. There are about 1,600 species of sea stars living today. Many species are about 8 to 12 inches (20 to 30 cm) across.

Sea stars usually have five arms that come from a central disk. The arms and disk are covered with short spines.

Sea stars eat sponges, clams, mussels, and coral polyps. They eat by pushing their stomachs out through their mouths. In the end, the sea star sucks its stomach and the **prey** back into its body. Sea stars don't have brains or blood. They have been known to grow new arms or even nearly whole new bodies, if needed.

CRUSTACEANS AND MOLLUSKS

Crustaceans are usually found in water. They're invertebrates, but have a hard outer covering called an exoskeleton. They have antennae and mouthparts. Crabs, shrimp, and lobsters are crustaceans. Crustaceans can be found in many parts of the ocean, including the sand at the base of coral reefs.

Creature Corner

Scientists have found more than 100,000 species of mollusks. They come in all shapes and sizes. Squid and octopuses are mollusks, too! Their shells are small and on the inside of their bodies.

The chambered nautilus is a mollusk that uses tentacles to catch its prey. Other mollusks filter, or take in and clean, the water to get food.

Mollusks are soft-bodied invertebrates. They have hard shells that cover their bodies. Clams, mussels, and oysters are common types of mollusks. They live in all parts of the ocean. In coral reef habitats, they attach themselves to the reef or hide in the sand.

REEF FISH

Coral reefs are home to more than 4,000 species of fish. About one-third of saltwater fish species live on coral reefs for at least part of their life. Coral reef habitats provide fish with shelter and food.

Parrotfish are brightly colored reef fish. They have a beaklike mouth they use to eat algae and the soft part of coral. Parrotfish can harm coral reefs.

Creature Corner

Some fish, such as the butterfly fish, trick their predators. They have markings that look like eyes near their tail. The predator bites their tail instead of their body, which makes it easier for the fish to escape.

14

Many reef fish, like this mandarinfish, are popular aquarium fish. However, this means that wild mandarinfish are in danger. Don't buy fish that have been taken from the ocean.

Damselfish are small, colorful tropical fish. Some damselfish live along reefs and others live in sea anemones. Damselfish are known for fighting over the place they live. They may chase away fish bigger than themselves, such as parrotfish.

PLENTY OF PREY

Many animals come to coral reefs to hunt their prey. Because so many fish and animals live on and around coral reefs, they are like an all-you-can-eat meal for larger fish such as sharks and rays.

Creature Corner

Sharks and rays sense their preys' movements using special sensing **organs** called ampullae of Lorenzini. These organs pick up on the tiny electrical fields other animals make.

Nurse sharks hunt for fish, shrimp, and squid. They also eat shellfish and coral.

Sharks hunt their prey using their senses. First they find their prey by smelling them or sensing their movement in the water. Then they **stalk** their prey before attacking. Sharks are able to sneak up on their prey because they are hard to see from above and below. Rays can't see their prey because their eyes are on top of their head. Just like sharks, rays hunt their prey using their senses.

SPEEDY SEA TURTLES

Seven species of sea turtles swim Earth's oceans. However, all species of sea turtles are found in warmer waters. Not all sea turtles live on coral reefs. Most sea turtles live in the open ocean and stop at reefs to find a quick meal. Sea turtles have a shell called a carapace. They can't pull their head or legs inside their shell like other turtles.

Sea turtles are speedy swimmers. They can travel up to 35 miles (56 km) per hour! Sea turtles spend most of their time underwater, but they must come to the surface to breathe and to lay eggs.

Creature Corner

Hawksbill sea turtles are the least plentiful species of sea turtles. This is because people have hunted them for their shells for thousands of years. People have used the shells to make jewelry, sunglasses, and other objects.

Hawksbill sea turtles live in the waters of the Atlantic, Pacific, and Indian Oceans. Their favorite food is sea sponges, which are found in shallower, or not deep, waters and near reefs.

BIG VISITORS!

Not all animals that live on or near coral reefs are small reef fish and crustaceans. Reefs get some big visitors! Dolphins and whales live mostly in open water. However, they come to reef habitats to find food. Dolphins eat small fish, squid, crab, and prawns. They hunt together in a group, called a pod, using noises to find their food.

The Great Barrier Reef off the coast of Queensland, Australia, is the world's largest coral reef. About 30 species of dolphins and whales visit the Great Barrier Reef.

Humpback whales are some of the largest coral reef visitors. They can be up to 50 feet (15 m) long and weigh up to 40 tons (36 mt)! These big visitors eat tiny sea animals called krill and small fish. Humpback whales only visit reefs in the winter months.

PROTECTING CORAL REEFS

Coral reefs are very important habitats. They're also easily harmed habitats. Damage from boats, pollution, overfishing, and taking coral out of the ocean can harm coral reefs. Coral reefs are also threatened as oceans continue to get warmer. **Bleaching** events can lead to entire coral colonies dying.

Coral reefs can't exist without coral polyps. We must do our best to take care of coral reefs. Use reef safe sunscreen when you go to the beach. Don't buy pet fish that have been taken from the ocean. Eat fish that have been caught or farmed sustainably, or go without eating fish. The world's oceans depend on us!

GLOSSARY

alga: Plantlike living things that are mostly found in water. The plural form is algae.

bleaching: When coral polyps get rid of the algae living inside them and turn white.

organ: A body part that does a certain task.

organism: A living thing.

prey: An animal hunted by other animals for food.

relationship: The way in which two or more people or things are connected.

shelter: Something that covers or protects people or things.

skeleton: The strong frame of bones that supports an animal's body.

stalk: To hunt slowly and quietly.

symmetrical: Having sides or halves that are the same.

tentacle: One of the long, thin, flexible parts that stick out around the head or mouth of an animal and are used especially for feeling or holding on to things.

tropical: Of or occurring in warm areas of Earth called the tropics.

INDEX

WEBSITES

Due to the changing nature of Internet links, PowerKids Press has developed an online list of websites related to the subject of this book. This site is updated regularly. Please use this link to access the list: www.powerkidslinks.com/wild/reef